PAWTUCKET
VOLUME II
IMAGES of America

This view of Main Street, Pawtucket in 1881 looks west past the junction with East Avenue and High Street. The serpentine lines in the middle of the street show the location of the horsecar track that superseded Whetherell & Bennett's and Sterry Fry's stagecoaches in 1864. The unusual curve in the track allowed horsecars to approach stepping stones placed in the often muddy road. The first building on the left is the John B. Read brick block, built in 1850. Next is William Tyler's house, followed by Ebenezer Tyler's three-story building. Across East Avenue is the Dexter Building which, in our day, housed the Slater Trust Company. The first building on the right is the Dr. John Gardner Estate, which later became Samuel Slater's second home. Across High Street is the LeFavour Block, followed by the Cleveland Mansion, the Lee Block—erected about ten years earlier—and the newly-erected Music Hall.

Cover: Finalists in the 1966 Miss Pawtucket Pageant take a stroll down Main Street in the business section wondering if they will be the one crowned Miss Pawtucket that night of May 6th at Tolman High School. From left to right are: Rosemarie Archambault, Christine M. Wojcik, Isabel McGreevy, Linda Ann Guatieri, Elaine Thibodeau, Nancy Bailey, Frances J. Dureault, and Linda Firth. (Photograph by James Hargreaves Jr.) See page 95 for the queen and her court.

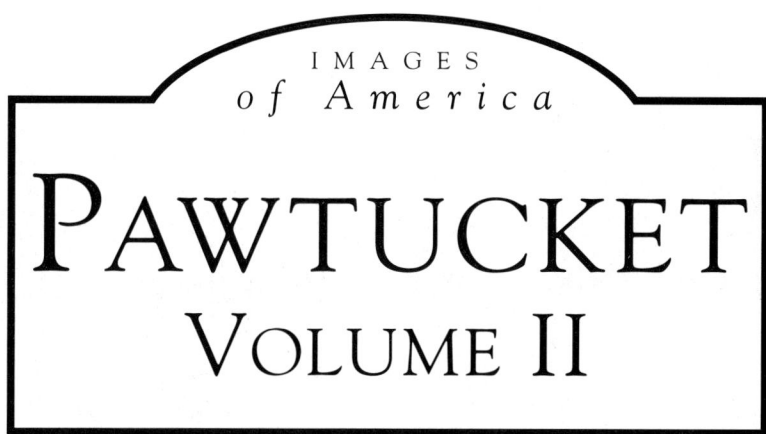

IMAGES of America
PAWTUCKET
VOLUME II

Elizabeth J. Johnson, James L. Wheaton,
and Susan L. Reed

First published 1996
Copyright © Elizabeth J. Johnson, James L. Wheaton,
and Susan L. Reed, 1996

ISBN 0-7524-0206-4

Published by Arcadia Publishing,
an imprint of the Chalford Publishing Corporation
One Washington Center, Dover, New Hampshire 03820
Printed in Great Britain

Library of Congress Cataloging-in-Publication Data applied for

This book is dedicated to the honor of Governor Joseph Jencks of Pawtucket, the first governor chosen from outside Newport. He served twelve years as Deputy in the General Assembly at Newport, four years as Speaker of the House of Deputies, five years as Major for Mainland Towns, five years as Assistant, thirteen years as Deputy Governor, and five years as Governor from 1727 to 1732. He was in the service of the town and state almost forty-four years.

What greater tribute can we present for such a life of service than to quote the words of American theologian, Jonathan Edwards (1703-1758) : "A man of right spirit is not a man of narrow and private views, but is greatly interested and concerned for the good of the community to which he belongs and particularly of the city or village in which he resides and for the true welfare of the society of which he is a man." Governor Jencks truly was that man of right spirit to whom we owe much for our heritage. (Governor Joseph Jencks oil painting by I. Smiberth, 1729.)

Contents

Introduction		7
1.	Going to Work	9
2.	Going Shopping	27
3.	Going to School	41
4.	Showing Respect	55
5.	Making Contacts	67
6.	Weathering the Elements	79
7.	Enjoying Pleasures	89
8.	Playing to Win	103
9.	Going Home	117
Acknowledgments		128

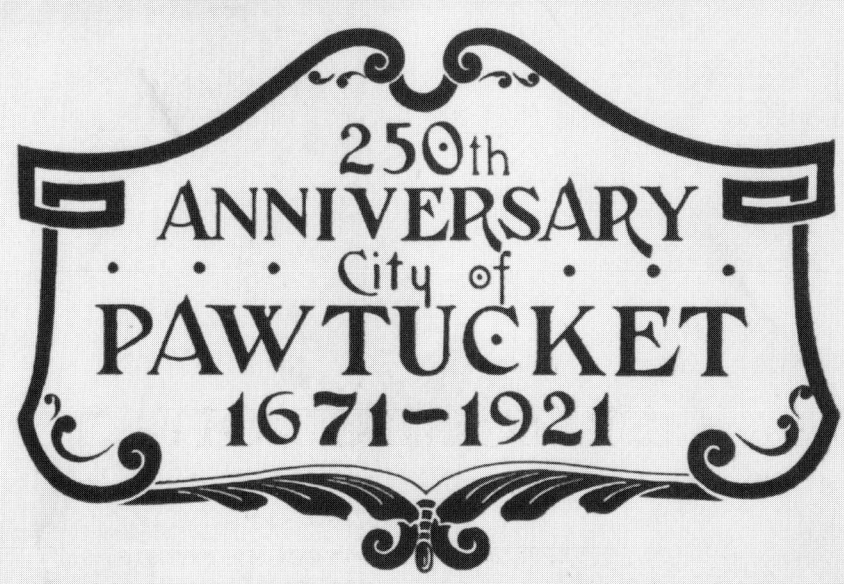

The Forge of Joseph Jenks, — 1671 — Founder of Pawtucket
FROM AN OLD PRINT

The 250th anniversary of the founding of Pawtucket by Joseph Jenks Jr. in 1671 was commemorated with this booklet. Joseph Jenks has the distinction of being the first white settler in Pawtucket. His energy and perseverance laid the foundation of Pawtucket, one of this country's greatest industrial centers. Attracted by the water power, Jenks purchased sixty acres of land lying near Pawtucket Falls from Abell Potter on October 10, 1671. Here below the falls, he built his forge, saw mill, and carpenter shop, and later operated an iron furnace and foundry. The forge was burned by the Indians in 1676 during King Philip's War but was immediately rebuilt.

Introduction

Selecting photographs for our 1995 publication, Images of America-*Pawtucket*, was very difficult because, with space restrictions, there was no choice but to exclude many photographs that we really felt worthy of inclusion. Images of America-*Pawtucket*, thanks to you, was a great success resulting in our being invited to author Images of America-*Pawtucket*, Volume II. This solves the dilemma. Photographs we had to exclude can now be included.

In this book, we have held somewhat to the same format and section subjects, but since today is tomorrow's history and because we want to capture the social flavor of our people, we have shifted emphasis quite slightly from nineteenth-century architecture to the people who created and molded Pawtucket, and to more twentieth-century images. It is our great pleasure to be able to share with you another collection of photographic treasures.

One
Going to Work

Pawtucket is the birthplace of the American Industrial Revolution. It was here that workers first left the farms to work in mills for an hourly wage. A natural outgrowth of that was the time card. Here we see workers lined up to punch their time cards in the company's time clock around 1920.

The Pawtucket Mutual Fire Insurance Company was located at 25 Maple Street. The right portion of this building was constructed in 1906 with an addition of equal size put on in 1938. The company was chartered in 1848 and began business in 1849 under the name Pawtucket Mutual Fire Insurance Company. It was originally located in the LeFavour Block on the corner of High and Main Streets. The first company officers were Edward S. Wilkinson (president), Captain John Tower (secretary), and Jesse S. Tourtellot (treasurer). The 1938 addition was designed by Monahan & Meikle, architects, and built for $94,000 by the A.F. Smiley Construction Company of Pawtucket.

This 1906 view of the main office of the Pawtucket Mutual Insurance Company reflects the solid, conservative image on which the company was founded, gained steady growth, and achieved an A rating. Current officers are James Hennessy (president), Vincent Del Nero (treasurer), and Leslie Harnish (secretary).

Located due west of downtown Pawtucket and straddling both Mineral Spring Avenue and the Moshassuck River, Lorraine Mills began as a brick mill for cloth and yarn manufacturing erected on the river bank in 1868 by C.D. Owens. Bought and incorporated as Lorraine Manufacturing Company in 1881 by W.C. and F.C. Sayles for the manufacture of cotton textiles, the original mill—now part of Mill No. 1—was soon surrounded by twenty-nine other buildings in which 2,800 people were employed. In 1882, manager James R. MacColl arrived from Scotland, and quickly the company's products became known worldwide for their quality. In 1897, a new worsted weave shed was added; in 1911 a yarn dye house was built; and in 1919, the company added a large finishing plant. James R. MacColl was succeeded by his sons William B. and Norman A. MacColl. Lorraine's progress was phenomenal under the MacColl leadership, and the Woodlawn and Fairlawn sections of Pawtucket developed directly as a result of that progress. A victim of the textile depression, Lorraine ceased production in October 1953. Today, the mill buildings are rented by small enterprises.

The Glencairn Manufacturing Company was founded in 1908 by John G. Brown at 5 Saunders Street at the corner of Cottage Street. The company produced silk shoelaces and cotton mercerized shoelaces (30,000,000 laces were produced per year). Braid and shoelaces continued to be manufactured at this location over the years. Brown once reminisced that "the biggest boom that ever hit the trade was right after World War I when women began wearing shoes up to the knee and needed two and one half yards for each shoe." Today, Glencairn is a division of the Rhode Island Textile Company (headquartered at 211 Columbus Avenue, Pawtucket), and is owned by its president, John "Jack" H. Elliot. The company also has a York Avenue division and operates plants in South Carolina and Mexico. (*Times* photograph.)

The Seekonk Lace Company, located on 2.75 acres of the Slater Park Plat at 659 Armistice Boulevard, owes its beginnings to William D. Sowter of Nottingham, England, who came to Pawtucket and interested several merchants in backing the lace plant. The company was organized in 1909 with one of those merchants, Henry J. Lynd of Lynd & Murphy men's furnishings, as its president. At the company's peak, it employed 250 workers. In more modern times, its president was the well-known philanthropist George R. Ramsbottom. The firm sold wholesale to intimate apparel concerns including Bali, Vanity Fair, and Playtex. In 1987, Seekonk Lace and its subsidiary, Rhode Island Lace Works of Barrington, were sold to Liberty Fabrics of New York, who closed operations in 1991 due to foreign competition. (*Times* photograph.)

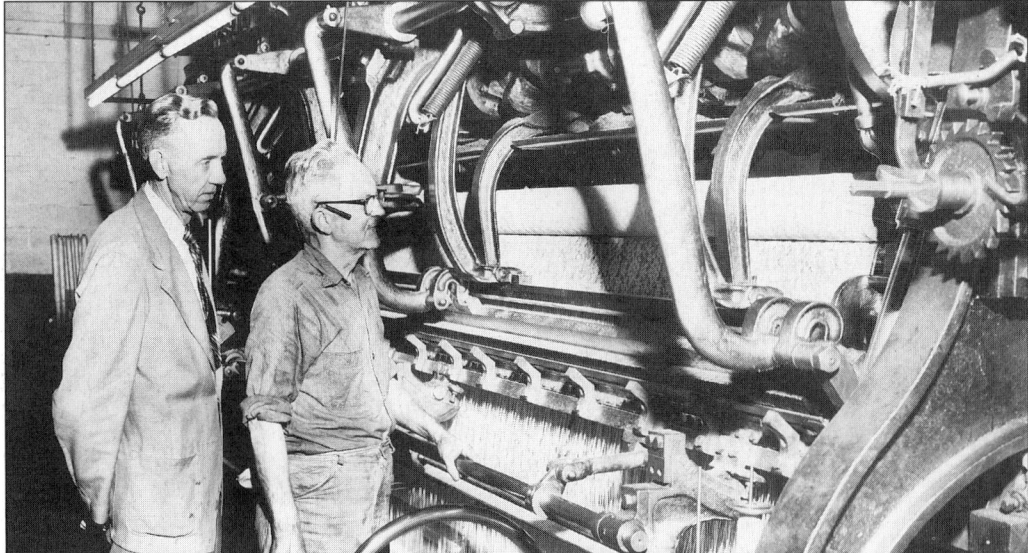

At the Seekonk Lace Company, James E. Gorman (assistant treasurer) and George Rondeau (weaver) tend to a huge Leaver Lace machine, the mainstay of the lace industry, in 1958. The company manufactured and finished fine to medium-grade laces including torchons, valenciennes, honiton, cluny, mattese, gimpure, nets, veilings, and others. (*Times* photograph.)

On Sunday, May 5, 1991, Pawtucket firefighters attack a blaze that destroyed an abandoned building formerly occupied by the Northeast Insulation Company at 333 School Street at the rear of the Pawtucket Medical Center. (*Times* photograph by Ken Love.)

In January 1996, Lieutenant Timothy McLaughlin, left, and firefighter Russell Renzi, right, test the Pawtucket Fire Department's new $399,850 ladder truck with its 110-foot aerial. The truck replaced the old Ladder One, the city's 85-foot aerial that was one of the last to use a tiller man—a driver who sat at the very rear of the truck to steer the back wheels. (*Times* photograph by Rich Dugas.)

Top left: Francis D. Morse, shown here, was born in 1830. He was co-founder, along with his son, Walter F. Morse, of the F.D. Morse & Son Book Bindery established in 1876. The bindery was in the Read Block at 94 Main Street (opposite today's Peerless Building, just renamed the Benjamin C. Chester Center). For many years, all city publications, including record books, reports, official pamphlets, and public library books, were produced by the firm known as "The Binders to the City." When Walter died in 1878, his brother Frederic A. Morse joined the company and carried on the business after his father's retirement in 1900. The firm moved to the Ellis Building on Broadway (the former unemployment office building) about 1925. The bindery was sold in 1933 to Mrs. Charles H. Potter, who moved it to the Smith Block on Main Street (approximately at today's Hodgson Park); the company was renamed the M.E. Potter Bindery, but was closed in 1941. Below: The office of the F.D. Morse Book Bindery as it appeared in November of 1893.

Brigadier General Herbert S. Tanner leads a Newport Naval Battalion, trained in suppressing street riots, from the Pawtucket Armory at Exchange and Fountain Streets in June 1902. After the riotous striking of street railroad employees, Pawtucket came under martial law. The affair was called Fitzgerald's Rebellion for Pawtucket's feisty Mayor John J. Fitzgerald, who sided with the strikers' demand for a maximum ten-hour work day.

Militia encamped in Goff Lots (at the corner of Fountain and Blackstone Streets behind Tolman High School and the Pawtucket State Armory) on June 12-22, 1902, during Fitzgerald's Rebellion. At its peak, the force numbered 641 (utilizing half of the state's militia), and included infantry, four Gatling guns, a number of cannon, and two riot-trained navy battalions from Newport. At the left rear is the American Yarn Manufacturing Company's brick mill (formerly the Richard Gage factory) at Fountain and Blackstone Streets. In the center rear is the Pawtucket High School (later Joseph Jenks Junior High School and now Doyle Manor). The houses on the right are along Fountain Street at May Street. All of these buildings are standing today.

The Tag Days event served as a means of soliciting money for worthy causes. This tag, printed by F.T. Sibley & Company, was sold in support of the Twin Cities Hospital on Park Place in Pawtucket. According to the November 27, 1908, *Pawtucket Gazette and Chronicle*, the results of the day were highly encouraging and the hearts of the people were in the right spot for this appeal for the aid of the suffering.

F.T. Sibley & Company is shown here in 1927 at 35 Humes Street. The company was established by Frank Tingley Sibley and George W. Bartlett at 224 Main Street in the Wheaton (now Toole) Building in 1891. It was moved to 65 Montgomery Street in 1916 and to Humes Street in 1927. Sibley died in 1936 and James L. Wheaton (father of the author) carried on his father-in-law's business until 1942 when World War II made it impossible to find employees.

The Troy Hand Laundry was established in 1875 by L.C. Smith. Charles F. Kinney became a partner in 1887 and later became sole owner. The laundry—shown here at 188 Exchange Street c. 1890—occupied land that is today a parking lot next to Morris Nathanson Design. In 1923, Kinney's son, C. Stanley Kinney, became a partner. In 1926, the Troy Hand Laundry was merged with other laundries to become the Colonial Laundry, located on Pawtucket Avenue.

John W. Little founded his printing business in Pawtucket in 1886 and, in 1914, erected this handsome brick factory at 190 Exchange Street at the corner of Fountain Street, the first all-electric printing company in the country. The company did extensive business in mill printing, gummed labels, sample cards, and tag making. Steven B. Little, grandson of the founder, sold this 101-year-old family business to Scott & Daniells of Portland, Connecticut, in 1987. In its later years, the company's accounts included Schick Safety Razor, Warner Lambert, Hasbro, and Pez. The company left Pawtucket in 1990 in search of larger quarters. (*Times* photograph.)

The Times Square Pharmacy was owned by druggist Wilfred A. Frigault. The pharmacy, opposite the *Times* Building, was opened in the Hall Building at 24 Exchange Street in 1941. Frigault's granddaughter, Elizabeth J. Smith (now Thresher), is shown serving at the soda fountain in 1950. The pharmacy closed in 1966 just prior to the demolition of the Hall Building for the construction of the downtown circulator highway. Today, the site houses the Social Security offices.

From left to right are: the Times Square Diner (1935-1975), the Home Café (1939-1960), and Ryan's Stationery/Book Store and Luncheonette (c. 1915-1957), which was originally William Ryan's newsstand. In 1957 when this picture was taken, Antonio Donati owned and operated the Times Square Diner and Abraham Rotman operated the Home Café. (*Times* photograph.)

On March 1, 1884, J. Milton Payne, Byron C. Payne, and George B. Olney organized the firm of Olney & Payne Brothers, one of Pawtucket's largest concerns dealing in coal, brick, lime, and cement. This 1897 photograph shows their large coal "pocket" (building) and dock opposite the state pier on the western side of the Pawtucket River just north of the gas company's tanks. Olney & Payne stayed in business until the retirement of Joseph Olney Jr. in 1980; in total, Olney served the city for ninety-six years. (Pawtucket Public Library photograph.)

The Bridge Mill Power Company generator room is shown here in 1912. This hydroelectric station, located below the falls at the Main Street Bridge, began operations May 1, 1896; in 1971 it was deemed inefficient and the facility closed. Escalating fuel costs since the 1973 oil embargo renewed interest in hydroelectric generating plants. In 1983, this station was placed on the National Register of Historic Places, and in 1985 it was reactivated to provide electricity for thousands of Pawtucket homes. (Pawtucket Public Library photograph.)

George E. Weavill, *Evening Times* circulation manager, poses with his drivers near the company's delivery truck fleet by the paper's loading dock on North Union Street *c.* 1960.

Weavill died in 1983. The Peerless Paper Company occupied the building in the rear in 1924. The building was torn down c. 1961/62. (*Times* photograph.)

Award winning-"ace" *Evening Times* reporter and WLKW radio news broadcaster, Mike "Digger" D'Ambra, chases a Pawtucket story *c.* 1964. D'Ambra retired in April 1990 after a forty-seven-year career at the *Times*. (*Times* photograph.)

Morris Earl "Flash" Dumin was an award-winning staff photographer with the *Pawtucket Times* for forty years. The friendly photographer has been described both as "one of the greatest *Times* goodwill ambassadors" and a "journalistic monk." A lifetime Pawtucket resident, Dumin retired in 1981 and passed away in 1992.

Howard B. Whitney, owner of the George L. Whitney Market at 111-113 Broad Street, stands in front of his store at its closing in 1957. Started by his father in 1902, the store catered to the "carriage trade" and had on its account books the names of most of the old and prominent families of Pawtucket, such as Goff, Ott, Read, Steele, Conant, Phillips, Thornton, Sheldon, Tingley, Jenks, and Bullen. The store's horses and wagons would set out between 7 and 8 am to take orders from the cooks and maids in the homes of the wealthy, and delivered those orders by noon. Howard always kept his father's name—"Geo. L. Whitney"—displayed prominently out front. (*Times* photograph.)

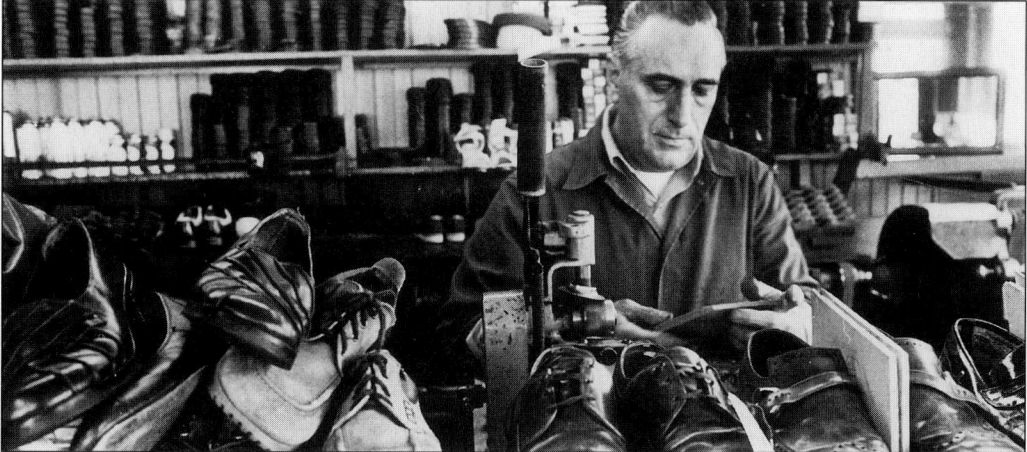

George Toste was mending soles and repairing shoes at the age of twelve. His father, George Toste Sr., an Italian immigrant, began business on Summer Street in 1914 and moved to this location at the corner of Summer and North Union Streets in 1935. Over the next forty-five years, Toste's became a landmark in Pawtucket. It became a shelter from the elements, a place to stop in for a few minutes to get out of the sun or rain and take a chair to sit or talk. In 1980, Toste moved his shoe repair shop from this latter location to his present workplace at 31 Exchange Street. (Pawtucket Public Library photograph.)

Here is the 1954 national sales staff of the Cooley company, manufacturers of awning fabric located at 50 Esten Avenue. From left to right are: (front row) Al deBedts (New York), Leo Ruff (Detroit), Phil Siener (Pawtucket), Bill Wilson (Pawtucket), and Gus Larson (Chicago); (back row) Arthur Leach (Pawtucket), Les French (Jersey City), Lawrence Mellor (Kansas City), Roger Gant and Glen Raven (both North Carolina), Bob Schofield (New York City), Joe Greco (New York City), Charles Bagley (Boston), Bob Siener (Pawtucket), Paul Eagleston (Chicago), Earl Wainright (Pawtucket), Tom Clarke (Jersey City), Rollin Sisung (Detroit), and Bill Griffiths (Jersey City).

The office of Collyer Insulated Wire Company was located at 249 North Main Street (now Roosevelt Avenue) between Exchange Street and Blackstone Street c. 1927. The typist at the far right is Bessie Flaxington (1901-1971), wife of Charles W. Fleming.

This building at the corner of Main and Maple Streets housed the Pacific National Bank (incorporated 1865, president, Lucius B. Darling); The Pawtucket Safe Deposit Company (incorporated 1865, president, Lucius B. Darling); The Pawtucket Institution for Savings (incorporated 1836, president, Hezekiah Conant); and on the fourth floor, The Pawtucket Business College (principal G. Milkman). The building, photographed here in 1897, still stands. (Pawtucket Public Library photograph.)

In back of the counter at the Pacific National Bank on 255 Main Street in 1894 are: (left side) William H. McKitchen (clerk), Frank L. Gatchell (teller), William J. Gatchell (clerk), and Charles L. Knight (cashier); (right side) George E. Nicholas (bookkeeper), Andrew E. Jenks (clerk), and George U. Tompers (clerk).

The William K. Toole Hardware Store, the inside of which is shown here in 1914, was founded in 1901 and incorporated in 1904. At that time it was located in the Read Block at 178-180 Main Street, now the site of 200 Main Street.

The William K. Toole Hardware Store was located at 76-88 East Avenue from 1925 to 1974. The company is still in business on Division Street. This photograph was taken on April 25, 1956, by the Roger W. King Company of Meriden, Connecticut.

Two
Going Shopping

Mildred Tingley opened her Little Acorn bookstore and gift shop on October 1, 1925. The store served multiple generations of Pawtucket readers. Tingley's motivation was expressed in her statement, "I've always thought of the selling of books and the giving of books as the scattering of acorns. . . . you never know what great oaks may come from them in the future." Mildred's sister Mabel (Tingley) Woolley ran the gift department. See also page 39.

During the early part of this century, Pawtucket native Robert A. Kendall (1849-1923) owned and operated The Capitol, a liquor and tobacco store at 221 Main Street.

This is the interior of Robert A. Kendall's Capitol liquor and tobacco store in downtown Pawtucket as it appeared in 1906. The store's patrons were the leading merchants and professional men of the city. Kendall carried a full line of domestic wines, whiskeys, cordials, and cigars and handled all brands of imported goods. The store sported a bar and employed six clerks.

J.E. Brennan & Company's drug store at 5 North Union Street in Trinity Square, shown here c. 1900, was opened in 1889 by Professor George Morgan and was known as Morgan & Shields originally. It was later known as Morgan's Pharmacy, and then the J.E. Brennan name took over. Leo Clark Sr. worked for Brennan and took over the store in 1921. Leo Clark Jr., who was the last to operate Brennan's, recalled the old soda fountain with a back bar and pumps. "My father used to slip some brandy into the milk shakes to improve their taste," said Clark. Brennan's "back room" used to be a favorite meeting place for the late Drs. Holt, Lynch, Wheaton, Rothwell, and Hughes, and pharmacists William Fortin and James Morgan. Brennan's hired a dozen people at a time and trained many a pharmacist. The store was closed in 1966.

The Sheldon Building, shown here in 1957, was built by Realtors Henry Herbert Sheldon and son Philip Collins Sheldon in 1886. It replaced an old house built by Maturin Ballou c. 1740 that was used as a tavern during the Revolution and later was known as the Miller Estate. The cornerstone of the Sheldon Building, which was inscribed "1740-1886," was the only piece of Diamond Hill granite found in the foundation of the old house. After changing hands several times, the building was purchased by the Pawtucket Redevelopment Agency from Sheldon Gerber in 1983 and razed to build the current China Inn. (*Times* photograph.)

The New York Lace Store, shown here in 1957, was founded in 1925 by Pincus Swetchkenbaum of Taunton, Massachusetts, and his sons Edward and Joseph. It was in the lobby of the old Bijou theater on Dexter Street near Trinity Square. Eventually the family expanded from the lace business into the ready-to-wear field, taking over the entire theater and moving into parts of the adjacent Taylor and Whipple Buildings. Concluding that no retail

store could hope to prosper without parking space and evening hours, they moved away from the downtown area in 1957. It was a sad day when they left their Broad Street location. Downtown Pawtucket has never been the same since. The Swetchkenbaums also owned Coats Field Shopping Center and the Warwick Shopper's World. (*Times* photograph.)

Alden R. Vaughn, born in Woodstock, Vermont, in 1851, established his watch-making and jewelry business in Pawtucket at 328 Main Street in the Lee Block in 1891. In 1919, he moved his business to his home at 69 Lyon Street where he took in repair business until his death in 1929. This photograph was taken in 1897. (Pawtucket Public Library photograph.)

This 1879 cartoon advertises the services of Herbert L. Edmonds, a manufacturing optician, whose shop was at 4 East Avenue near the corner of Main Street. Cartoons and caricatures of this type are highly sought after as collectors' items.

Bernard McCaughey & Company (Jeremiah Leahy, partner) used this delivery wagon for their house furnishing business, established in 1884. The driver's name is unknown. Born in Lismore near Claugher, County Tyrone, Ireland, in 1844, McCaughey arrived in New York in 1865 with $12.50 in his pocket. He opened this business in what had been the old horsecar barn at 73-78 North Main Street (now Roosevelt Avenue) at the corner of Slater Avenue near the police station. The business needed more space and moved to East Avenue in the Slater Trust Bank Building in the early 1900s. In 1921, McCaughey built his own building just across East Avenue from the Boy's Club.

The grand opening of the new, imposing Bernard McCaughey & Company store at 60 East Avenue at the corner of Timothy Street took place in April 1921. Every window was filled with flowers sent by friends. Added to this was a photograph of Bernard McCaughey, the founder, who died just one year earlier, and many flags and twining ivy. Ten thousand visitors visited that afternoon and evening. McCaughey's daughter, Sadie McCaughey, closed the business at this site in 1927 and moved around the corner to 11 Timothy Street. Adams Furniture occupied the building in the 1940s.

1875 – 52nd ANNIVERSARY 52nd – 1927

We are 52 years old June 17th, 1927.
We are a Rhode Island Company, started and owned by Rhode Island People. We have been serving the house-keepers of Rhode Island with Groceries continuously for 52 years.

Nicholson-Thackray Co.

Fig Bars, Anniversary Price, 3 pounds for 29c
The favorite Crispo Brand.
One carload just received fresh from the factory.
(Regular price 3 pounds for 38c)
Buy a carton of 9 to 10 pounds at the lower than ever price.

Campbell's Tomato Soup, Anniversary Price, 3 cans for 22c
(Value 10c can)

Chipso, for clothes, for dishes. Anniversary Price, 19c
The popular large package. (Regular price 22c)

Seeded Raisins, Anniversary Price, 2 for 19c
Large 15-ounce packages. (Regular price 13c)

Roger Williams Fancy Chili Sauce, Anniv. Price, 2 for 25c
8-ounce bottles. (Regular price 16c bottle)

Grape Fruit, Blue Ribbon Brand, Anniversary Price, 19c can
(Regular price 25c)

California Peaches, Anniversary Price, 12c can
Sutter Club, No. 1 cans. (Regular price 15c can)

Hires Root Beer Extract, Anniversary Price, 18c bottle
(Regular price 23c bottle)

Hatchet Maine White Corn, Anniversary Price, 13c can
(Regular price 18c can)

Tyler's Coffee Syrup, Anniversary Price, 20c bottle
Makes fine Milk Shakes. Can be used for many other purposes.
Children are very fond of it in milk. Try a bottle at this special.
(Regular price 25c)

NEW   TOPS-ALL BOILED HAM   NEW
To introduce, Anniversary Week, Tops-All delicious Boiled Ham. 30c for a half pound package of lean, sliced Ham all cooked ready to serve. Easily 40c value.

Corned Beef Hash, Prudence Brand. Excellent for a rush meal.
Big cans, 29c can
P. & G. White Naphtha Soap, 6 bars for 25c
Asparagus Tips, Square Cans. Very tender. Eagle or Hillsdale
Brand. New low price, 28c can
Leslie Popular, small, sweet, tender Peas. New low price, 18c can
Portland Maine Sweet Sugar Corn. Very low price, 2 cans for 25c
Campfire Popular Peaches. New low price, 25c can
Hawaiian Sliced Pineapple, Lei Girl, large cans, 23c can
Haffenreffer's Sparkling Brew, Contents, 4 bottles for 25c
Clicquot Club Golden or Pale Ginger Ale, Contents, 2 bottles for 25c
Quaker Quick Cooking Oats, large packages, 24c package
Roger Williams Pineapple Jam, 25c jar
Roger Williams Tomato Ketchup, 12c and 18c bottle
Red Bag Popular Genuine Ceylon Tea, 59c pound

Nicholson-Thackray had forty grocery stores in the city of Pawtucket in 1927 (the time of this advertisement).

Delivery wagon #2 gets ready to deliver groceries and baked goods in 1906 from Nicholson-Thackray's 338-342 Main Street store across from today's Old Colony Bank Building. One of Nicholson-Thackray's features was the prompt delivery of all orders.

William Harrop's drug store at the Four Corners in Woodlawn (the intersection of Lonsdale and Mineral Spring Avenues) is visible at the center of the background of this photograph. The photographer was standing where a McDonald's is today. The store, started by Dr. James A. Robinson in 1892, became Beaudry and Harrop by 1902. In 1907, Louis Philippe Beaudry was listed as a physician and Harrop was left alone at the drug store. Harrop went out of business after his death in 1963. Today this spot is the location of the John B. Santos Park. This photograph was taken in 1917.

Joseph J. Flynn was a cigar maker in Pawtucket as early as 1898. He and his brother James began their family business at 44 Mason Street under the name of James Flynn & Company in 1904, the year this picture was taken. Jim and Joe "Jimanjo" continued the business through 1918, when they were located at 394 East Avenue. They advertised themselves as "manufacturers of Union Made Cigars - Ten cent cigars and private brands a specialty."

Peter Tarpy, son of owner Martin Tarpy, nudges hind quarters of beef toward a delivery truck while Steve Lennon guides the process from below the loading dock at Tarpy's Wholesale Meat House at 71 Dexter Street in 1970. In 1923, Martin Tarpy's father Stephen Tarpy became a partner with John K. Bateman to form Bateman & Tarpy. Their 71 Dexter Street building was constructed that year. Bateman died in 1936 and the business was then known as Tarpy's. Tarpy's closed in 1994, idling twenty-two employees—a great loss for Pawtucket and the food industry.

This photograph was taken in 1965, when the city anticipated turning downtown Main Street into a shopping mall. This part of Main Street looking west from East Avenue was to be closed to vehicular traffic under the Blair Report Proposal. This attempt at being competitive with suburban shopping centers proved unsuccessful and consequently, Main Street now has one-way vehicular traffic. (*Times* photograph.)

The two-story brick building at North Union and Summer Streets, shown here in 1963, once housed the offices of the Pawtucket-Blackstone Valley Chamber of Commerce. The chamber owned the building and leased space on the ground floor to three businesses. Most of the luncheon meetings and workshop sessions were held in rooms on the second floor. Today, Tom's Restaurant is in the lower level at 29 Summer Street. (*Times* photograph.)

The Davis Florist Shop at 1 Alfred Stone Road was started in 1915, the year of this photograph, by Fred S. Davis, superintendent and treasurer of the Riverside Cemetery. Davis's wife, Carrie May Davis, operated the flower shop after her husband died in 1937 and continued the business until 1961 when she was eighty-nine. The building still stands. The handsome brass marker that is shown on the side of the delivery truck now graces the cemetery office of Polly (Davis) Stiles, granddaughter of Fred S. Davis.

The Tingley sisters, Mildred Tingley and Mabel (Tingley) Woolley, moved their Little Acorn bookstore and gift shop from North Union Street to this location at 33 Broadway in 1948, around the time this picture was taken. In 1959, they again moved, this time to the LeFavour Block at the corner of Main and High Streets. In 1966 they made their final move to Park Place, where they sold only books. They retired in 1968. Appropriately, an endowed fund awards two scholarships each year, the "Little Acorn Scholarships," to two graduates of the Pawtucket high schools (one male, one female) who attend Brown University. See also page 27.

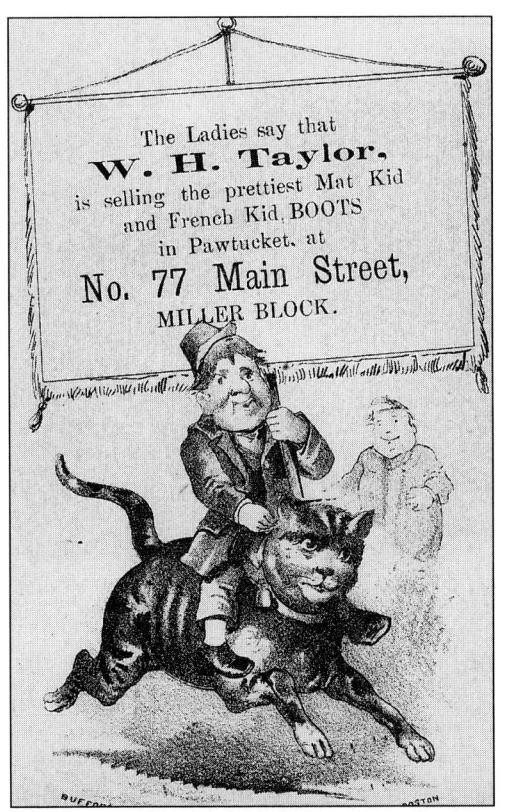

An 1876 caricature advertises W.H. Taylor's shoe store, then located in the Miller Block at the corner of Main Street and Mill Street (now Roosevelt Avenue). Taylor came to Pawtucket *c.* 1870 and purchased the shoe store of Brooks & Merriss at the corner of Main and High Streets in the old Slater Homestead. Taylor died in 1892.

In 1894, the David Harley Company's Boston Store moved into the new four-story Conant Building at the corner of Main Street and Park Place opposite today's downtown parking garage. The building is shown here in 1897. In 1901, the building was doubled in size. It was doubled again in 1912. More than 125 persons were employed here. This building has been replaced and now houses the registry of motor vehicles. (Pawtucket Public Library photograph.)

Three
Going to School

The Pawtucket elementary school children heading for home from the Fallon Memorial School on Lincoln Avenue in March 1991 are, from left to right: Jason Simao, Raymond Brown, Sari Mann, and Ryan Dooley. (*Times* photograph by Antoine C. Boulanger.)

The Cherry Street School Kindergarten Cottage, built in 1896 at 23 Cherry Street at a cost of $6,300 including a piano and other furniture, was the first public school kindergarten cottage in New England. A. Mabel Perkins was the teacher and Nellie E. Lawton was assistant in this novel experiment. In 1922, the abandoned school building became the home of Pawtucket Post No. 4 of the American Legion. It was destroyed by fire in the 1960s.

Schoolchildren were at work in the Cherry Street School Kindergarten Cottage garden in 1911. The garden was located on a lot owned by Mrs. Olive M. Ormsbee at 32 Cherry Street. Teachers believed that an outdoor work project in the garden would serve as a basis for classroom lessons in spelling, numbers, drawing, and nature study. Weekly instructional visits were made by E.K. Thomas of the Kingston Agricultural College (now the University of Rhode Island).

Melissa Pinleiro and Ryan Saint Germain of the Woodlawn Catholic Regional School—poster winners and national finalists in the U.S. Department of Energy 1992 Earth Day Poster Contest—proudly display certificates of merit presented by Rhode Island Governor Bruce Sundlan. Woodlawn Catholic Regional School was formed in 1972 as a result of the consolidation of the Maria Goretti, Saint Jean the Baptist, and Saint Edward's Schools. (*Times* photograph by Rich Dugas.)

"Queen of the Crosswalk" Joan Reis lets students from the Potter-Burns School safely cross busy Newport Avenue in January 1990. Reis was on the job from 1977 until her retirement in July

1990. (*Times* photograph by Rich Dugas.)

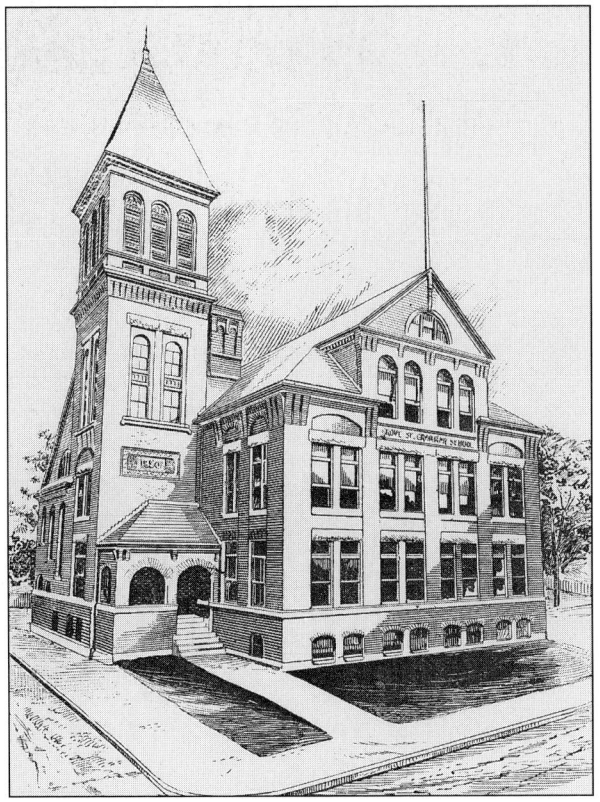

The original wooden Grove Street Schoolhouse was built by contractor James Gilmore Briggs in 1843 and contained four classrooms. It served for forty-eight years. The building was sold at public auction for the sum of $37.

Built on the same foundation, this nine-room Grove Street Schoolhouse replaced the old wooden schoolhouse shown above. It was dedicated on September 3, 1891. The architect was William R. Walker & Son. Mason work was done by J.L. Bryant, carpentry by Wilmarth & Mackillop, and plumbing by J. Sewell Read. An addition was built in 1908, doubling the school's size, and the city open-air class moved into the building in 1931. The building was torn down in the 1960s and the land was used as a parking lot. Condominiums now occupy this land at Grove and Spring Streets.

The Our Lady of Consolation School on Webster Street, built under the leadership of Monsignor Joseph Claver Bessette at a cost of $60,000, was dedicated in 1904. It accommodated about five hundred children who were taught by eleven Sisters of Sainte Anne. Three years later these teachers were replaced by the Sisters of Sainte Chretienne. Once known as a French school, it today serves students with many ethnic backgrounds from Pleasant View to Rehoboth, Cumberland, South Attleboro, Providence, and Lincoln.

The talent winners from Pawtucket's Donna Carter Dance Studio in November 1994 are: (at bottom) Charisse Draleau; (on the stand from left to right) Justine Shelton, Tiffany Heroux, Erin Livingston, Andrea Yattan, Natasha Cestaro, and Melanie Periera. (*Times* photograph by William Huntington.)

Side by side in this 1968 photograph are the old Lincoln Avenue Schoolhouse and the new Lincoln Avenue School (now Fallon Memorial) just before demolition of the historic building. School histories show that the old school building was built in November 1895 and the new one in 1950. But what none mention is the fact that the 1895 building replaced a still older schoolhouse built in 1879 and destroyed by fire in February 1895. The first school was "a two story affair with one room on each story and was used for the first, second and third grade." The teacher in 1879 was Nellie M. Bradley, and the teacher at the time of the fire was Sarah L. Cullen.

Fallon Memorial School sixth-graders paint a dinosaur mural. From left to right are: Lakeesha Craig, Malanie Desmaris, Michelle Miller, unknown, and Viveka Ayalla. (*Times* photograph by Rich Dugas.)

Principal Robert E. Moran discussed a writing lesson with Martha Normandin's 1989 third-grade class when he was principal at the Elizabeth Baldwin School. Moran is now principal of the Fallon Memorial School. (*Times* photograph by Earl Dumin.)

Principal Albert L. Copeland looks on from the rear. The librarian at the desk was Mabel L. Short. The Samuel Slater Junior High School on Mineral Spring Avenue opened its doors for the first time on September 9, 1925. One thousand pupils from six grammar and elementary schools were enrolled.

These students were honored in September 1993 as grade-level winners in the summer reading contest at Our Lady of Consolation School in Pawtucket. From left to right are: (front row) Steven Jackson, Theresa Peters, Derek Oliveira, and Lacy Smith; (back row) Michael Fournier, Shaun Cooley, and Billy Jackson. (*Times* photograph by Rich Dugas.)

The menu in this 1925 view of the Slater Junior High School cafeteria appears to have consisted of hot dogs, hamburgers, pudding, apples, and milk.

The Slater Junior High School seventh-grade class of 1992 enjoys a pizza party in the cafeteria. The 225 students in attendance may be vividly contrasted in style and appetites with their counterparts of 1925, shown above. On the left is Peter Silva, second from the left is William Ingram, on the right is Jerome Cosme, and second from the right is Jose Resendes. (*Times* photograph by Rich Dugas.)

David Clark, the instructor wearing a suit coat, bow tie, and apron, directs this 1925 class in electrical wiring at Samuel Slater Junior High School.

Contrast Clark's class above with that of instructors Charles Antonian (wearing a jacket) and Peter Michaud in 1993. The two men are shown helping seventh-grader John Packer in the new computer room at Joseph Jenks Junior High School. (*Times* photograph by Rich Dugas.)

In 1989, the swimming pool at Tolman Senior High School was being made available for the Hollywood cast and crew of the movie *Mermaids*, starring Cher. (*Times* photograph by Rich Dugas.)

Founded nearly thirty years ago, the New England Tractor Training School (NETTS) operates out of 10 Dunnell Lane. Truck fleets from across the country send recruiters to hire the school's students.

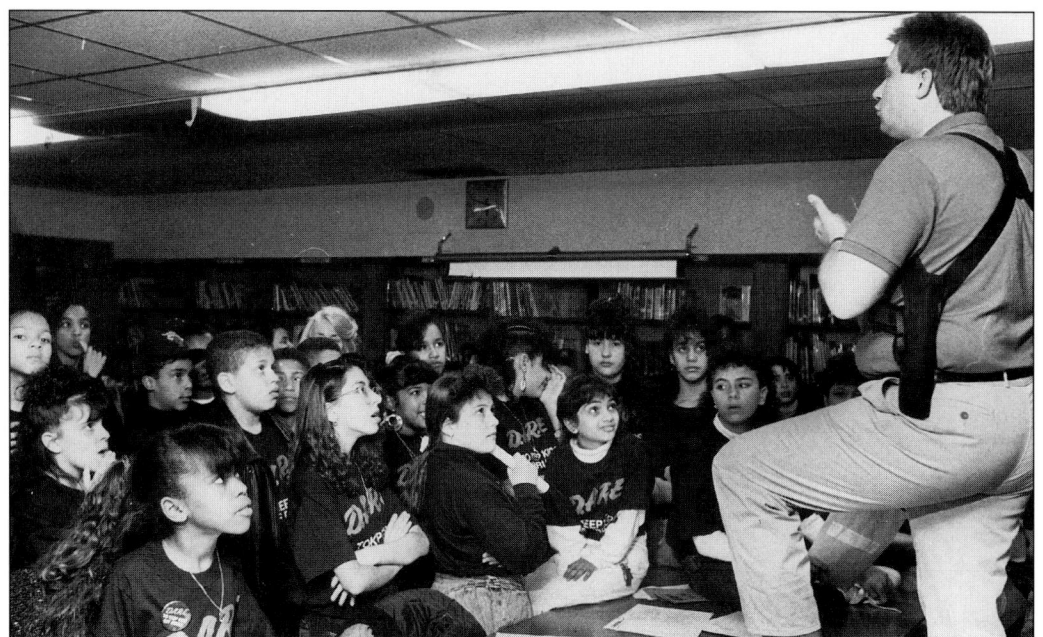

Officer Ed Warzycha gives last-minute instructions to D.A.R.E. (Drug Abuse Resistance Education) graduates of the Cunningham School in 1992. The D.A.R.E. program, made available to all sixth-graders in the city, was established by officer Gil Arundale six years earlier to help young people identify and resist peer pressure that might lead them to alcohol, smoking, drugs, or fighting. Every kid knew Gil and called him by name. "He made the program work." (*Times* photograph by Antoine C. Boulanger.)

Shea Senior High School students exercise their civic responsibilities in 1993 and get their message across with a banner. From left to right are: Heather Larivee, Chantelle Brown, Jessica Rubinacci, Danny Baptista, and Hugo Teixera. (*Times* photograph by Bill Gucfa.)

Four
Showing Respect

Kelley Square, at the corner of Smithfield Avenue and Weeden Street, is dedicated to the memory of PFC Robert J. Kelley, USMC, killed in action in Okinawa on May 16, 1945. Sponsored by the Elwood J. Euart VFW Post, the square was dedicated on June 27, 1971.

Grand Army Hall, at the corner of Exchange and Hamilton Streets, is shown here c. 1895. The building was originally built as the third building to be used by the Universalist church. In 1867, an armory facade was added, as seen in this photograph, and the building was called the Tower Light Battery Armory (later it was called the GAR Hall). The facade and front portion were removed in the early 1900s to facilitate the widening of Exchange Street. The John E. Fogarty Home for the Elderly occupies the site today.

The armory, above, was used during 1861-1865 by a unit of the U.S. Sanitary Commission—the Civil War equivalent of the USO. Girls and women in hoop skirts rolled bandages and assembled small articles of clothing and other comforts for the soldiers and sailors at the war fronts. (Pawtucket Public Library photograph.)

Trinity Church, Episcopal, was begun in 1843 with meetings in the American Hall on lower Broadway. Ground was broken for this church building on Main Street on August 30, 1847, by its first minister, the Reverend James Cook Richmond. The building was consecrated on July 12, 1853. It exists today as Saint George's Marionite Church at 50 Main Street.

The Reverend James Cook Richmond, founder and first rector of Trinity Church, Episcopal, is shown here in 1847.

The gates to Riverside Cemetery, 726 Pleasant Street, are shown here in 1891 before Alfred Stone Road was built. Just inside the gates is a charming Late Victorian Gothic cottage built for the use of the cemetery manager. The wooden gates have been replaced by gates of brick and iron, but the cottage still graces the entrance today.

Edwin McDermott, who has worked diligently for years restoring and documenting Old Saint Mary's Cemetery, studies this monument to James E. Wilson. Wilson was a Fenian and Irish patriot who spent the last portion of his life in Central Falls and Pawtucket following a daring escape by sea in 1876 from a British penal colony in Freemantle, Australia, in which he played a key role in leading nine others to freedom.

This monument that honors the unknown dead of the Civil War was dedicated on Memorial Day, 1902 in Mineral Spring Cemetery by the Tower Relief Corps. There are twenty-eight markers in the oval plot of land surrounded by an iron fence.

This imposing soldiers' memorial monument at Wilkinson Park in Park Place honoring all who served in the Civil War was dedicated on May 31, 1897. It was the result of eleven years of diligent planning by the Ladies' Soldiers' Memorial Association and its president, Mrs. James L. Wheaton. It is the work of sculptor W. Hastings Granville titled *Liberty Arming the Patriot*.

This American Flag Unit, composed of 250 school children dressed to represent the American flag, marched on Main Street in the Founder's Day parade on Monday, October 10, 1921, which celebrated the 250th anniversary of Pawtucket.

This arch, on downtown Main Street at today's Roosevelt Avenue, was built by volunteer carpenters including Mayor Kenyon and Captain William McGregor, chairman of the anniversary committee. The arch, titled "Labor's Offering," bore the official greeting to all visitors to Pawtucket during the city's 250th anniversary celebration which ran from October 8-12 in 1921.

This postcard depicts the 1906 Saint Jean's Day parade marching south on High Street between Exchange and Main Streets. The old post office, currently the library annex, is shown in the left background. It is the only one of the buildings still surviving. The old First Baptist Church is on the left and the High Street Methodist Church can be seen on High Street in the far back of the picture.

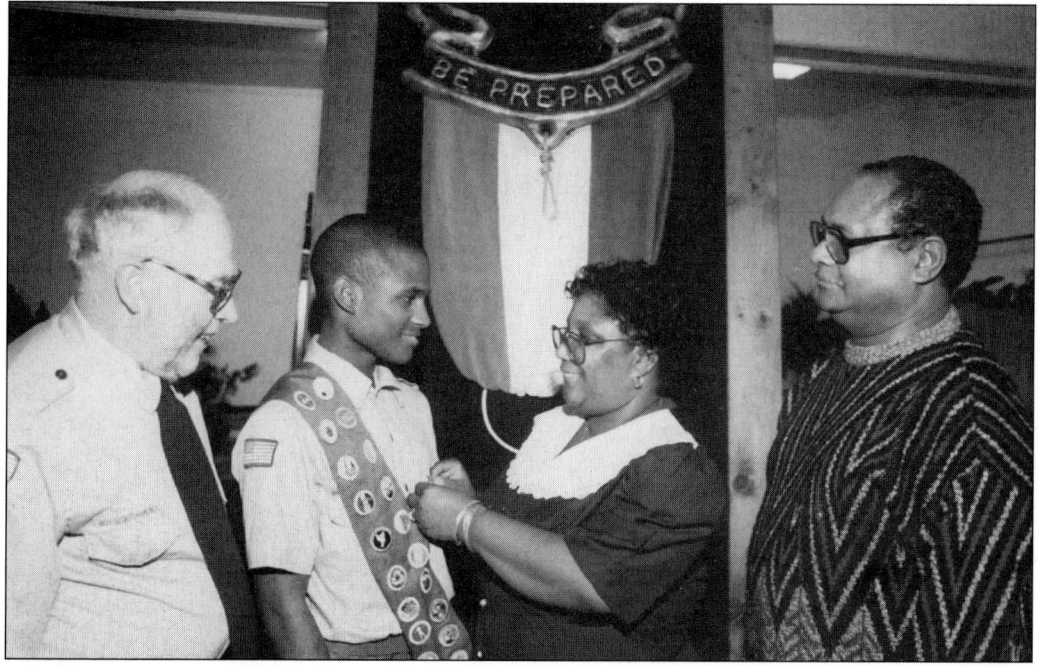

Curtis Brown of Boy Scout Troop #24, Pawtucket receives his Eagle Scout Award at the Union Baptist Church at 50 Lupine Street on November 6, 1993. Looking on are scoutmaster George Anderson, a scout leader since 1973, and parents Betty Brown and George Rogers (who has since passed away). (*Times* photograph by J. Supancic.)

Pawtucket's 1921 Armistice Day parade float by the American Legion depicts the part America

played in World War I. (Photograph by Chester W. Goward.)

The Church of the Advent was started as a bible study group in members' homes in 1873. The group later assembled in a house on Lowden Street. In 1879, they were affiliated with the Episcopal church. In 1884, a chapel was erected on the corner of Pawtucket Avenue and Trenton Street. In June 1894, the congregation was admitted into union with the Episcopal Diocese as the Church of the Advent. In 1915, the church was enlarged and had 200 students in Sunday school and 265 members overall. It continues today, 123 years after its first meetings were held.

Begun by members of the Baptist church in Central Falls as a mission Sunday school in the old East Street School in Pleasant View in November 1867, the Pleasant View Baptist Sunday School Society moved to the Atlantic Engine House on Carnation Street in 1868. On April 10, 1876, the group moved into their new chapel on land on Fountain Street opposite Gooding Street donated by manufacturers Greene and Daniels. The congregation became the Pleasant View Baptist Church in 1880. The building was enlarged in 1887. In 1925, the church burned. It was rebuilt and dedicated in 1930. The name was changed to the Memorial Baptist Church in 1935. The church building was demolished by the construction of Route I-95. In 1961 the congregation merged with that of the Hebron Baptist Church. The two groups' combined Memorial Baptist Church in Seekonk, Massachusetts, was dedicated in March 1963.

The Woodlawn Baptist Sunday School began on July 4, 1875. The church was organized in 1893. In August of 1893, the Reverend Whitman L. Wood began his service as the church's first pastor and continued for twenty years. The church building shown at the corner of Lonsdale Avenue and Weeden Street was occupied in 1902. The building, after all these years, still serves this vibrant congregation.

A Capeverdean-American Community Development (CACD) team heads out for a neighborhood cleanup on Slater Street in July 1994. The adult team leader is Paul Gonsalves, a Pawtucket police officer. (*Times* photograph by William Huntington.)

Five
Making Contacts

Three-year-old Tyler John Jutras picks out some new books from the Pawtucket Public Library's children's section for his grandmother, Rose Jutras (in the background), to read to him. This photograph was taken in 1994. (*Times* photograph by Jennifer Smith.)

This 1890s view shows the Pawtucket City Hall on the east side of High Street just south of Summer Street. The structure was built in 1871 by what was then the Town of North Providence as a secure and fireproof place for keeping town records. It served as city hall until 1936 and then afterwards housed a military recruiting station, the war rationing board, and the draft board. The building was torn down in 1968 during urban renewal.

The Pawtucket Board of Aldermen held sessions in the old Masonic Temple next door to the city hall in early 1929. From left to right are: William Knott, William Margerison, Joseph Williams, Peter Keough, Mitchell Adams, and Alfred Gobeille.

Judge Anthony Dennis presided over the Fifth District Court in Pawtucket City Hall just after a complete overhaul in 1984. The business of this court is now handled in the Providence Sixth District Court. The city hall facilities now house the Pawtucket Municipal Court, where zoning, housing, and traffic violations are heard.

Lieutenant Kenneth Gendron shows off new holding cells in the remodeled Pawtucket Police Station. The scene today looks pretty much the same as it did in this April 1984 view. (*Times* photograph.)

The annual concert and ball of the Pawtucket Fire Department was held in the Music Hall in downtown Pawtucket. Music was provided by the American Band with D.W. Reeves conducting. The sixteen-page program, the cover of which is shown above, was very unique. The cover depicts Foreman William Titus, in full uniform, striking the alarm at Box 35 near the Mineral Spring Cemetery. A $1 ticket admitted one gentleman and two ladies. A ladies' ticket was 50¢.

Four thousand people enjoyed this affair. The concert was given in the Leroy Theatre and the dance in Payne Hall next door. "The fact that the large drill shed at the armory with its uneven dance floor had been abandoned for a modern playhouse and up-to-date pavilion was a source of much enjoyment," according to a newspaper account of the day.

Voting Supervisor Tillie Vascovitz looks over the voter list at Francis J. Varieur Elementary School on Pleasant Street during the October 1993 primary election. (*Times* photograph by Rick Kelley.)

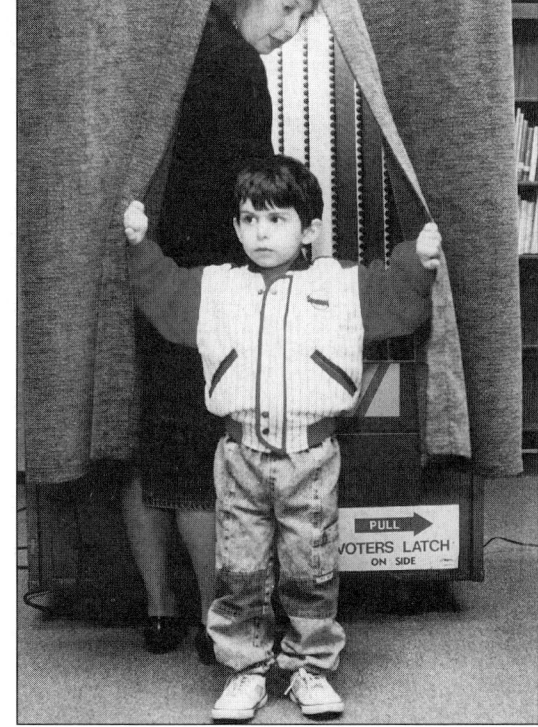

Henry Barcohana, age four-and-a-half, pulls open the curtains to the voting booth while his mother, Esta Barcohana of Pawtucket, tries to make her selections at the Varieur School in the October 1993 primary election. (*Times* photograph by Rick Kelley.)

Jim Robbins poses with the fire department's new rescue boat in October 1988 outside his auto body repair shop at 1153 Central Avenue. (*Times* photograph by Rich Dugas.)

The South Woodlawn or West Avenue Fire Station was built in 1912 with a facade of "pattern-brick" at a cost of $24,125. The architect was Robert C.N. Monahan and the contractor was Frank G. Rowley. This fire station is the last original one still in service in Pawtucket—a real candidate for preservation.

In this unique photograph from Mayor Robert E. Metivier's personal files, President Clinton is presented a PawSox hat and shirt while on the stump in Pawtucket in November 1994. Clinton was the third president to visit Pawtucket; the other two presidential visitors were James

Munroe (who came in 1813) and Andrew Jackson (who came in 1833). From left to right are: Mayor Robert E. Metivier, Mrs. Carol Metivier, and President William "Bill" J. Clinton. Representative Patrick J. Kennedy is shown in the background.

The Elks Building at 27 Exchange Street was built in 1927 at a cost of $150,000 by Pawtucket Lodge No. 920, Benevolent and Protective Order of Elks, in their twenty-third year. The three-story yellow brick and cast stone lodge and commercial building was executed in the Spanish Renaissance style. One of the building's first tenants was the Kissel & Kissel Kar dealership. Today, in addition to the Elks, it houses the City Nights Dinner Theatre and other ventures. The Elks, eight hundred strong, are now planning to relocate within Pawtucket to a place where they can enjoy a more cost-efficient building that affords better parking.

The constant double-parking game outside the Pawtucket Post Office on Montgomery Street is illustrated vividly here during peak rush-hour congestion in September 1955. The game persists today! (*Times* photograph.)

Titled "New Irish American Hall" in this December 1929 photograph, this brick building replaced a cottage at 62 North Union Street purchased ten years earlier by the Irish-American Building Association. The earlier building was let to various other societies including the Ancient Order of Hibernians Ladies Auxiliary, Modern Woodmen of America, and C.W. Hawes Camp No. 9450. The original trustees were: John J. Crawley, James Doherty, Michael McAloon, Thomas Sheehan, William Murray, Timothy Foley, and Thomas Hunt. The 1929 building committee members were B.H. Keenan, Thomas E. Hand, and James Doherty. The building stands today with the modern facade of the former Equitable Credit Union. (*Times* photograph.)

A group of thirteen young men with an interest in keeping boys off the street and out of trouble organized the Novelty Park Club at a shack on the corner of Division and Tyler Streets in 1914. The club was non-political, non-partisan, and non-sectarian. No man was too big or small, too humble or lofty to become a member. The club was famous for organizing marathons, carnivals, block dances, a legion post, a boy scout troop, and a polling place. The group later built a wooden structure that was replaced in 1922. Above, the cornerstone for the new structure is being laid. The club folded in the early 1940s and the building burned in 1961. Today, this land contains the Lan Mar Apartment Building on Division Street and the Tot Park on the Johnson Street side. (Pawtucket Public Library photograph.)

In 1921, this brick recreation building at 457 Lonsdale Avenue overlooking the Coats Athletic Field was erected by the J. & P. Coats company for the benefit of its employees. The building contained a restaurant seating 2,000, an entertainment hall, bowling alleys, pool tables, and baths. In 1981, after serving as Coats Shopper's World (shown here in 1970), the building was renovated, with no major architectural changes, to house twenty-six apartments as part of Coats Manor. (*Times* photograph.)

The YWCA of greater Rhode Island built this new school age child care facility at 324 Broad Street in 1991 to keep pace with the changing needs of the community's women. (*Times* photograph by Antoine C. Boulanger.)

Six
Weathering the Elements

The words on this historical marker near Roosevelt Avenue on Exchange Street quote the words of the great Narragansett Chief Miantonomi, who described the northeast corner of the land grant he gave to his friend Roger Williams, who then settled Providence. (Pawtucket Public Library photograph.)

The Freshet of 1886 dumped heavy and continuous rains on February 11-12. In all, 8.13 inches of water fell. This plus snow melt caused one of Pawtucket's worst floods. The Slater Mill was but an island after the unfinished dam at Diamond Hill Reservoir washed away pouring its contents into Abbott Run and then into the Blackstone River. All day Saturday and Sunday crowds from here and neighboring towns converged on the Main Street Bridge as seen above. Spectators had to be kept moving to give everyone an opportunity to view the scene.

Ice collected in the river below the Main Street Bridge in late February and early March of 1886, producing what were called "ice gorges." The so-called gorges created the appearance of "snow blown into windrows and thrown up by railroad plows and furrowed by teams - a rough surface of snow-ice," according to a newspaper account. Happily, the rising tide broke up this ice jam quickly.

The Pawtucket Congregational Church at the junction of Walcott Street and Broadway is shown here in the 1890s. In the immediate right foreground is the historic second Slack Tavern at what is now the entrance to School Street. See also page 124.

The spire of the Pawtucket Congregational Church (see above) crashed into Broadway as a result of the Great Hurricane in September 1938.

An old battered craft and debris line the shore near the state pier off School Street after Hurricane Carol on August 31, 1954. Saint Mary's School can be seen on the heights above the river's west bank. (*Times* photograph by Levin.)

This extensive damage to the Newell Coal and Lumber Company just south of the Division Street Bridge on the west bank of the Pawtucket River was caused by Hurricane Carol in August 1954. The arrow points to a man on a tractor almost lost in the rubble. (*Times* photograph.)

The raging water of the Blackstone River passes the Old Slater Mill during a spring freshet on March 25, 1969. (*Times* photograph.)

Fountain Street lived up to its name on Sunday, November 28, 1993, during a storm in which heavy rain and winds up to 40 mph whipped through Pawtucket. (*Times* photograph by Bill Gucfa.)

The Blizzard of '78 is seen looking east on Main Street from Park Place. (*Times* photograph.)

The sign says it all at the Union Wadding Company at Goff Avenue during the Blizzard of '78. (*Times* photograph.)

What a beautiful day emerges as the sun begins to hide behind the clouds but still glistens in the Pawtucket River. The view is seen from the Old State Pier looking west toward the Valley Resources gas armatures in May 1989. (*Times* photograph by Rich Dugas.)

It's shirt-sleeve weather! Dennis Millet walks down Broadway in record-breaking heat on January 1, 1995, with his son Dennis III (age one-and-a-half) and daughter Brittany (age four). (*Times* photograph by Bill Gucfa.)

A cold spell in late January 1994 had frozen parts of many waterways, as these hockey players discovered on the Pawtucket River in the Bishop Bend section of the city. (*Times* photograph by Rich Dugas.)

Bob Cash enters his sanding truck at 2:45 pm on January 11, 1995, in time to make city streets safe before rush hour. (*Times* photograph by Bill Gucfa.)

Pawtucketites make their way along Exchange Street at Broad Street during the Blizzard of 1996. The Centennial Tower housing unit can be seen in the background. (*Times* photograph.)

Sustained gale-force winds in February 1996 ripped scaffolding from the former Peerless Building, now the Benjamin Chester Building. This view is of High Street looking south toward Main Street across from the Tavares Newsstand. The Toole Building can be seen on the horizon on Main Street. (*Times* photograph by Bill Gucfa.)

Seven
Enjoying Pleasures

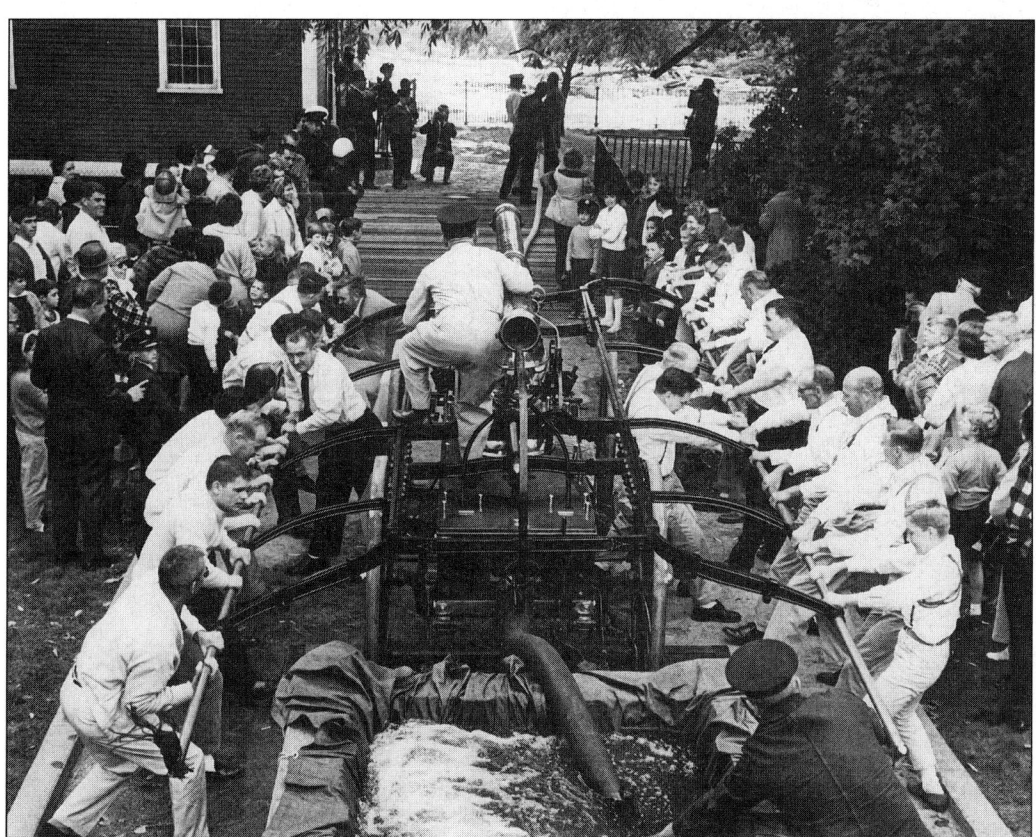

Squirting a stream of water from this ninety-two-year-old hand pumper, the Washington No. 1 from North Kingstown, was a feature of a fire exhibition program called "Three Centuries of Fire Fighting" held at the Old Slater Mill in September of 1966.

The bandstand on the north side of Central Pond in Slater Park was designed in 1917 by architect Robert C.N. Monahan and built by contractors Wilmarth & Mackillop. It is of granite composite construction with a Ludowici shingle-tile roof. It is 24 feet in diameter and provides 460 square feet of floor space. An inscription bearing the names of composers Reeves, Godfrey, Pryor, Sousa, Innis, Creatore, Cappa, Gilmore, Brookes, and Herbert surrounds the frieze. Many a summer Sunday afternoon was spent enjoying band concerts here.

The Bungalow at Slater Park was designed by Robert C.N. Monahan and built in 1909. It was an open-air pavilion for resting or waiting for a rain shower to end. It was torn down in 1984 due to vandalism and disrepair.

The boathouse at Slater Park, shown here in 1917, was originally constructed as a gift of James C. Potter, chairman of the park commission, in 1917. First known as the "Potter Casino," the structure was designed as a field house, boathouse, and sanctuary (or rest house). The architect was Robert C.N. Monahan. The building was idled after a fire ended its use as a community theater in 1980. It underwent a $75,000 renovation in 1984, afterward becoming the new home of the Rhode Island Water Color Society.

Brian Marsolais of Pawtucket, age five, is shown sliding with his sister Heather, age eight, at the Slater Park playground in July 1993. (*Times* photograph by Omar Bradley.)

Pawtucket Boys and Girls Club Members of the Month appear here in February 1991. Roger Tavares (left) and Carlos Rendon stand for their picture in front of the 1902 plaque commemorating the gift of the Boys Club building by Lyman Bullock Goff in memory of his son, Lyman Thornton Goff (1868-1900). (*Times* photograph by William Huntington.)

This is the Robinson, Green & Beretta architectural rendering of the $2.5 million Alfred Elson Jr. Branch of the Pawtucket Boys and Girls Club on School Street. It was dedicated August 30, 1988. Governor Licht arranged to purchase the former Naval Reserve Center for $35,000, and Dr. Gary P. Paparo, president of the club, accepted the offer to buy it from the state for the same price. (*Times* photograph by Antoine Boulanger.)

Albert M. Bertozzi's Narragansett Bowling Alleys opened in 1942, remaining in business at 820 Newport Avenue until 1952. Today, the Susan Montgrain School of Dance stands on this site.

The gala opening of the Darlton Theatre on October 22, 1940, featured two grand productions: *Maryland* with Walter Brennan and *We Who Are Young* with Lana Turner. The theater closed in the fall of 1978, and was burned by vandals that December. This building at 810 Newport Avenue was owned by Robert G. Pinault, whose father, William B. Pinault, had it built. C. Reuben Moberg was the architect. (Photograph by Warren Jagger.)

The fourth annual business meeting and banquet of the Pawtucket Merchants' Association took place on January 7, 1903, in the Maple House on Maple Street in downtown Pawtucket. In the front on the left is Bernard McCaughy of the McCaughy Furniture Company and seated second from the front on the right of the table is the organization's president, Fred L. Smith of the Fred L. Smith Plumbing & Heating Company. The men had just heard the great news that the state would spend $1,000,000 to improve the street railway, grade crossings, and telegraph service in Pawtucket.

Seated on the big bass drum in 1909 is Pawtucket's future radio and film star, Nelson Eddy (1901-1967), who was then living at 57 Lyon Street with his grandfather. He was making his first public appearance as a boy soloist singing "The Lost Chord" with the Coast Artillery Band at Fort Greble (now Dutch Island) off the coast of Jamestown, Rhode Island. Standing behind him is his father, William Eddy. His grandfather, Isaac Eddy, is seated to the left of the drum.

Miss Pawtucket 1967, Vera Jacinto, poses with her court at the pageant on May 7, 1966. From left to right are: Linda Ann Guatieri, Elaine Thibodeau, Jacinto, Linda Firth, and Christine M. Wojik. Other contestants are featured on the cover. (*Times* photograph.)

Karen Jutras, Pawtucket native, Tolman graduate of 1976, and daughter of Jack and Millie Smith, won the Mrs. Rhode Island International 1995 title and went on to compete for the Mrs. America title in Texas that August. (*Times* photograph by Rick Kelley.)

The Sons of Father Mathew, a temperance organization in Pawtucket from 1896 through 1931, sponsored this award-winning flute and drum band. Father Theobald Mathew, an Irish Franciscan priest, twice brought his total abstinence crusade to Rhode Island in 1849 following

his success in London in 1843. Father Mathew spoke to large crowds at Saint Mary's Church in Pawtucket in October of 1849. The organization was last located at 63 High Street next to the old Masonic Temple. (*Times* photograph.)

Persons often had their portraits taken with their prized possessions. This *carte de visite* of an unknown young girl with her rocking horse, taken c. 1864, was found in a Jenks family photograph album. Advances in photography around the 1860s made the production of multiple prints from one negative possible for the first time. This accounts in part for the popularity of the *carte de visite*, which was used as a calling card

Marjorie A. Bradshaw, author of *The Doll House-Story of the Chase Doll*, published in 1986, is shown here with Chase dolls from her own collection. Chase dolls were the product of Martha "Mattie" Jenks (Wheaton) Chase, the wife of Dr. Julian Chase. Mattie made her first stockinette doll in 1889 just for family. The doll-making grew into a business located in "The Doll House" behind the Chase home on Park Place; Mattie supplied stores around the country and eventually even sold dolls to hospitals for use in training medical personnel. Today these dolls are valuable collectors' items. (*Times* photograph by Earl Dumin.)

Author Jim Wheaton appears c. 1942 at home at 58 Greene Street, where his Easter chicks grew to laying hens, much to the chagrin of the neighbors. There are none more fresh than backyard eggs.

These youngsters splash around in the first formal test of the water at Dunnell's Pond, the municipal swimming hole on Prospect Street near Prospect Heights, on July 3, 1949. In 1984, a new athletic complex was located on the 13 acres of filled land that had been Dunnell's Pond. (Pawtucket Public Library photograph.)

The gypsies are in town! Here at 59 Water Street, c. 1920, gypsies had moved into a storefront and hung old bedspreads and sheets in the front windows to make their new home more private, as it was common for them to do.

Lovely's Diner at the corner of East Avenue and Church Street was the place to go after the movies in the 1930s. Second from the left is James Lovely and seated on the stool is Joseph Lovely. Young Joe Lovely, of another generation, was forced to move from downtown by urban renewal and the Downtown Circulator. In 1967, he relocated to 200 South Bend Street near McCoy Stadium, where the historic diner continues today. The photograph above was taken on August 30, 1931.

Lieutenant Richard Foland of the Pawtucket Fire Department poses with Pepper, the mascot of the Roosevelt Avenue Fire Station, at city hall in April of 1986. (*Times* photograph.)

George W. Kent and his daughter Ruth are off on a 1914 trip to Europe in their own car driven by James Kinnell, who was later a teacher in Pawtucket schools and father of Galway Kinnell, Pawtucket Hall of Famer. The twenty-six room Kent Mansion was built in 1904 at 744 Benefit Street and was torn down in 1938. Its 23 acres today comprise the Pinecrest section of Pawtucket.

By contrast with the photograph above, this July 1992 picture of little Kerri Lamoreaux of Pawtucket shows her rolling down Smithfield Avenue in a spiffy new mini-jeep. (*Times* photograph by Ken Love.)

Eight
Playing to Win

Despite blistering heat, some 5,000 spectators turned out to watch this July 1989 PRO-AM bicycle race in Pawtucket. The annual race featured top-level amateur and professional competition. (*Times* photograph by John Supancic.)

Members of the J.C. Potter team, eastern Pawtucket elementary school baseball champions, were rewarded with a June 22, 1921, trip to Fenway Park in Boston to see the Red Sox and Yankees. In between halves of a double header, the boys played two innings against each major league club. During the contest, Babe Ruth purposely stumbled to first, allowing young Harry McGuire to throw him out. Said McGuire: "I had thrown out the greatest hitter in baseball!" The Potter team, shown here surrounding the Babe, included Earl Nolte, Pete Truchon, Rhody Hart, Billy Breault, Phil Callahan, McGuire (seated cross-legged on the right in the front row), Harold Olden, Bobby Reid, and Albert Legare. Also in the picture are Joe Sullivan (the Potter team's business manager), Henry Winters (wealthy Texas promoter of boys' sports), "Stuffy" McInnis and Herb Pennock (Sox players), and Mike McNally and Bob Shawkey (of the Yanks).

Top right: Les Pawson won the April 1933 Boston Marathon in the record time of 2 hours, 31 minutes, and .6 seconds. (*Times* photograph.) Below: Les Pawson, who won the 1933, 1938, and 1941 Boston Marathons, shown here in 1982, ran well into his eighties. The Pawtucket and Rhode Island Hall of Famer died at eighty-seven in 1992. (*Times* photograph.)

Horse racing became an integral part of Pawtucket with the opening of Narragansett Park on Newport Avenue in 1934. This scene in the winner's circle was a daily occurrence. Enjoying a win at "Gansett" Park in 1974 are, from left to right: Larry Calabro, Nino Calabro (trainer), unknown, and Ernie Hutton (groom).

In the historic match race that attracted national attention, Alsab is shown defeating Whirlaway by a slim margin at Narragansett Park on September 19, 1942, before a crowd of 40,000. The finish of the race is superimposed over the crowd.

Starters ready the starting gate at Narragansett Park in April 1978. (*Times* photograph by Earl Dumin.)

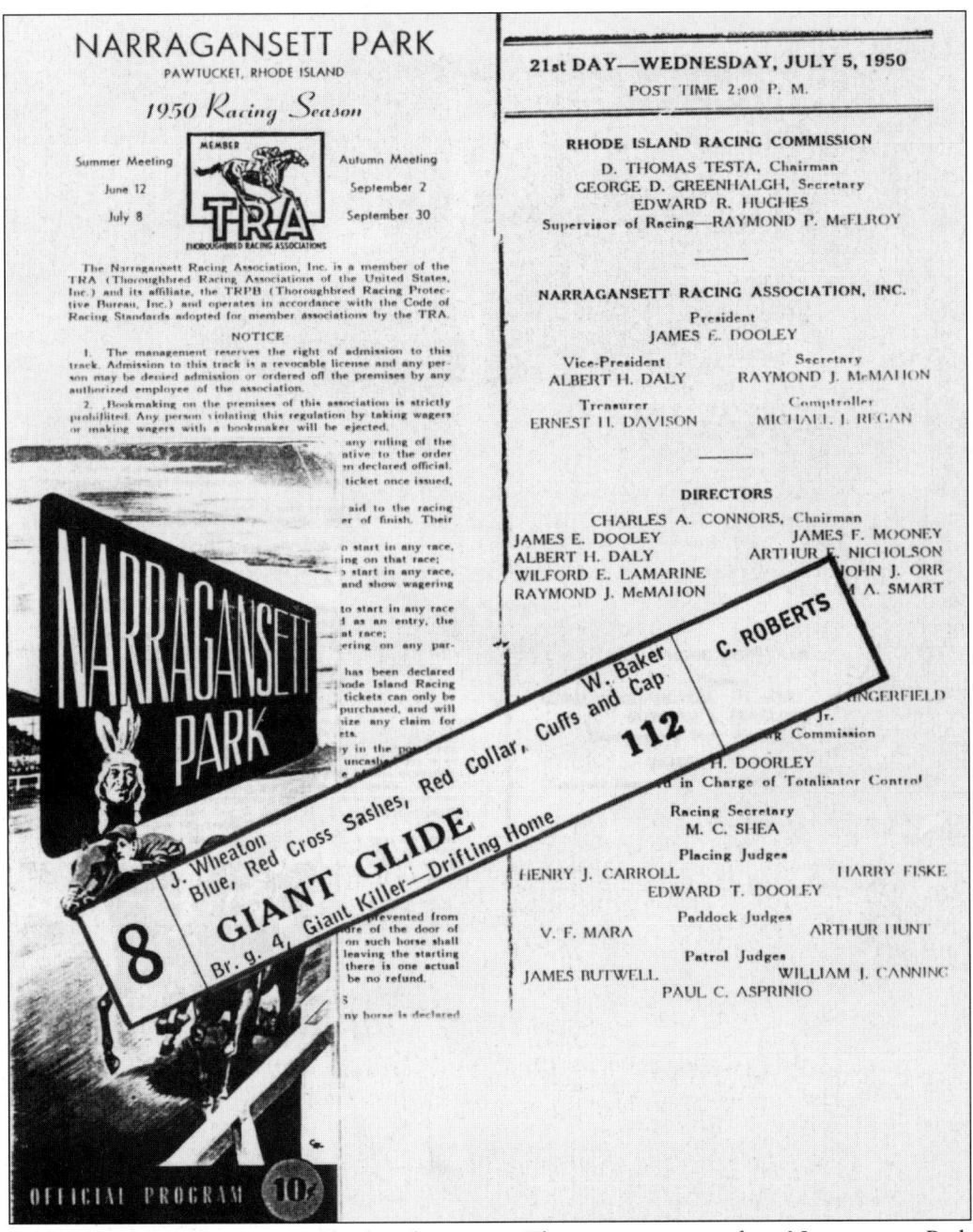

Even author Jim Wheaton tried his hand at racing. This racing program from Narragansett Park on July 5, 1950, shows his entry of Giant Glide that day. J. Wheaton is listed as owner, W. Baker as trainer, and C. Roberts as jockey. If I remember right, we came in last.

Originally named the Pawtucket Public Arena, Pawtucket's fine new ice skating rink replaced six houses on Beatty Street from the corner of Mason Street. Built at a cost of $700,000 and opened in January 1974, it was destroyed by fire on October 1, 1978. After a $314,000 restoration, the arena was renamed for Mayor Dennis M. Lynch and reopened exactly one year after the fire. This is a 1994 view.

The Dennis Lynch Arena has produced many a champion skater. Here, during the 1991-1992 season, the Fine Line Precision Skating Team, sponsored by the Pawtucket and Providence Skating Club and the Pawtucket Parks and Recreation Division, poses for the camera. From left to right are: (front row) Pamela Supernard, Anne Casey, Michele Scalin, Stacy Burgess, Bethany Merry, Michele Proulx, Renee Beaulieu, Kerry Pontes, Erin Gouin, and Jennifer Taveres; (back row) Jennifer Parker, Susan Goulet, Laurie Swisher, Kelly Swisher, Susan Godlewski, Erin Zawacki (coach), Lynn Midgely, Laurie Pickles, Janice Maynard, Michele Hardy, and Mary Ann Harrison.

An April 1987 view from the 18th fairway of the Pawtucket Country Club provides a picturesque sight for golfers hitting their approach shots onto the 18th green. The country club was built by Monahan & Meikle in 1923 for $26,038. (*Times* photograph by Rich Dugas.)

This warm Saturday in 1991 brought golfers out to the Pawtucket Country Club. Here we see Cliff Crowther about to tee off; the others in his foursome are Ted Tavernier, Frank Dipiro, and Byron Quinn. (*Times* photograph by Ralph E. Smith.)

Lawn bowling became a part of Slater Park in 1983 when members of the Slater Park Lawn Bowls Club transformed a dump behind the Slater Park Carousel into a 160-by-160-foot bowling green. Pictured here in July 1992 is Paul Bucklin of Attleboro making a serious effort at the East Division Lawn Bowling Championships held at Slater Park. Looking on is Alfred Letourneau of Pawtucket. (*Times* photograph by Ken Love.)

At the Slater Park tennis courts in 1991 are, from left to right: (front row) Matthew Cournoyer and Krystal Noiseux; (back row) Sharon Wishnevsky (instructor), Sandy Novak, Lisa Novak, Andrew Gugel, and Heidi Hartzell (assistant instructor). (*Times* photograph by Bill Gucfa.)

In October 1994, the Kiwanis Club presented a check to the Barton Street Community Center for a boxing ring. From left to right are: Manny Rodrigues (an eleventh-grader at Central Falls High), Raymond "Red" McCarthy and Raymond J. Dumont (past presidents of Kiwanis), Bill McCaughy (Kiwanian), Charles "Chuck" Sczuroski (director of the youth center), and Junior Pires (a Central Falls High senior). The center was developed by the Pawtucket Police Department's Community Police Unit to help a neighborhood, besieged for years by drug dealing and prostitution, take back control of their community. (*Times* photograph by Bill Gucfa.)

The Boston Red Sox "Splendid Splinter," Ted Williams, drops in on PawSox owner Ben Mondor during the summer of 1990. (*Times* photograph by Antoine C. Boulanger.)

Max W. Read, beloved director of physical education at Tolman High and coach of many championship swimming teams, congratulates young Paul Flynn of Prospect Heights, age eleven, who had just won the fifth grade race for boys at Dunnell's Pond on July 28, 1949. Max was then swimming director at the pond.

The 1923 Pawtucket High School swimming team members were, from left to right: (front row) unknown, Chet Caulfield, Charles H. Lawton, William Arthur, and Ralph Mills; (second row) Charles Fleming and other unknown young men.

This 1988 photograph is of George Patrick Duffy, perhaps Pawtucket's premier all-around sports figure of the 1900s. During his career, Duffy tried his hand at hockey, football, baseball, basketball, and boxing; was publicist for the Providence Steamrollers basketball team and many other sports teams; entered the minor league operations of the Boston Braves and Cleveland Indians; was a slow-pitch softball manager, player, and promoter; served as a coach in both city high schools, CYO, and semi-pro basketball; and was a television and radio broadcaster, providing play-by-play at the college and professional sports levels. Among Duffy's many honors is his election to the Pawtucket Hall of Fame. (*Times* photograph.)

The 1967 Cadet Baseball champions were from Saint Teresa's of Pawtucket. Here they are shown with Monsignor Daniel J. Ryan. From left to right are: (front row) Garry O'Brien, John Cullinan, Joseph Braganca, and Thomas McLane; (middle row) Wayne Perry, Greg Murphy, Bill Mulholland, and Joseph McIntyre; (back row) Paul Rankowitz, Joseph McCoy, Greg Caffrey, Joseph Gamba, and Bill Heany (coach). Seated in front is the bat boy, Mike Heany.

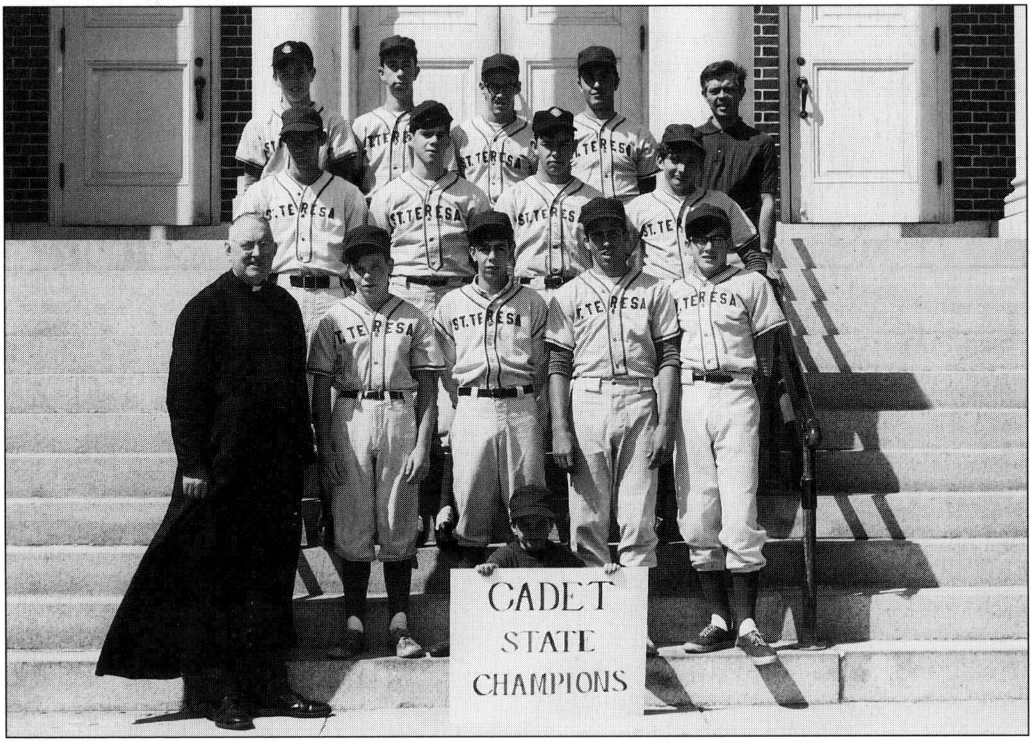

Chester R. "Chet" Nichols was noticed by the Boston Braves for his outstanding pitching at Pawtucket East High School and was signed in 1949. As a major league rookie in 1951, Nichols posted the best earned run average in the National League with a mark of 2.88. Chet won eighteen games for Vancouver in the Pacific Coast League during a comeback in 1960, and started the All-Star game. He also pitched for the Milwaukee Braves, the Boston Red Sox, and the Cincinnati Reds before retiring in 1964. In 1989, he was pitching coach for the Baltimore Oriole's Class A team in Bluefield, West Virginia; in 1990 he coached their Class AA pitchers in Wausau, Wisconsin. He persuaded Ben Mondor to purchase the Pawtucket Red Sox and was the team's vice president. Chet Nichols Field in Lincoln honors his accomplishments in baseball and his philanthropic service to his community.

The Pawtucket Celtics soccer team had just returned from their trip to Puerto Rico in May 1988. Fred McKinnon, a fifth-grade teacher at Fallon School and former Acting City Recreation Director, initiated a soccer program and selected a team of fourteen to seventeen year olds to compete by invitation in Puerto Rico. From left to right are: (front row) Joseph Mulhearn, John Claudio, and Alfredo Rose; (middle row) Michael Godek, Albert Noddings, Russell Godek, and Jose Anbuquerque; (back row) Fred McKinnon, James Medeiros, Richard Mulhearn, Orlando Andrade, Manuel Vincent, and Thomas Valentine.

Sam Clogston of Olcott, New York, moves his boat *Firefly* along the dock at the Old State Pier off School Street as he prepares for competition at Pawtucket's August 1995 Steamboat Muster. (*Times* photograph by Rich Dugas.)

Nine
Going Home

Each window and car wheel in this c. 1910 postcard represents a scene from Cumberland through Central Falls to Pawtucket. Note the Cumberland Town Hall in the left window, the Jenks Park tower in Central Falls in the center panel, and the post office (now the library annex) in Pawtucket on the right.

Edward E. Bucklin (1870-1940), hackman, is about to drive his wagon up East Avenue Hill (now relocated) on his way home to 33 Wayland Street (now Sayles Avenue) off Pawtucket Avenue in 1892. The house in the foreground, 108 East Avenue, was the home of Alexander H. Cross. The lodging house in the rear was that of Thomas H. McCusker at 4 Pleasant Street.

Bumper-to-bumper traffic had accumulated on Exchange Street at the junction of High Street in 1959. Facing east on the right is the Exchange Street Bar, the United Public Market, and the Fuller Jewelry Company (just over the Exchange Street Bridge). Across from that, the state armory can be seen on the skyline. (*Times* photograph.)

In 1991, "nice guy" neighbor Ernest Brassard of 190 Francis Avenue built this beautifully-crafted tree house for the kids in his area. From left to right are: unknown, Steve Degnan, Justin Pray, Steve Parent, Dacia Pray, and Matt Degnan. (*Times* photograph by Rich Dugas.)

This was the residence of Benjamin and Anna I. (Oatley) Gridley from 1909 until Benjamin passed away at age ninety-eight in 1959. Gridley drew design plans for many mill buildings and power plants in this country, particularly in the local and New England areas.

This picture captures the living room of the Gridley House (shown above).

The McCormick apartments and market at 221 Walcott Street were built for John McCormick of 2 South Bend Street in 1925 by the O'Malley-Fitzsimmons Company. The structure is a three-story, flat-roofed, "pattern-brick" apartment block with one street-level storefront. Handsomely detailed, it is very well preserved.

The Joseph Spaulding House at 30 Fruit Street is the home of author Betty Johnson and is the first private residence in Pawtucket accepted on the National Register of Historic Landmarks. Built in 1828 by cabinetmaker Joseph Spaulding, the house has been carefully restored. The Spaulding House Research Library for Pawtucket history has been developed within its walls.

The R.C.N. Monahan House on Denver Street was built for Robert C.N. Monahan of Monahan & Meikle, architects. It is a two-story Shingle style cottage. Its gambrel roof flows forward to encase a front porch. A rotund corner tower is marked by a cobblestone first story and wide-eaved conical roof. It is a whimsical design for an architect's own home.

This 1932 home of architect Robert R. Meikle at 16 Sayles Avenue on Oak Hill Plat is a more conventional Cape Cod style, five-bay, one-and-one-half story house with a gabled roof—totally different from the home of Meikle's partner-in-business, Robert C.N. Monahan, shown above. However, its informality includes the fine detail of its living room and clubby-den retreat with pine paneling in the rear.

Above: This drawing by Bob Gumley is of the Fifth Ward Room at 47 Mulberry Street, one of two remaining polling places built when Pawtucket was incorporated as a city in 1886. The building was later used as a school and still later as a legion post. In 1980, Mr. & Mrs. George Jerry made creative use of the vast interior space. The brick and granite building sports large arched windows with a playful arrangement of mullions separating the window panes. Below: The "Great Hall" of the Jerrys' converted Ward Room (shown above). (*Times* photograph by Earl Dumin.)

The home of Dr. James L. Wheaton, great-grandfather of the author, is shown in 1892 just prior to being removed to make way for the brick building that is today the Toole Building on Main Street between Park Place and East Avenue. Originally built c. 1732, it was the home of distiller of rum, James Sheldon, and his wife Diadama. The house was then owned in succession by merchants Nathaniel Croade and Bosworth Walker. James Wheaton and his son, Dr. James L. Wheaton Sr., bought the "Walker House" in 1864. It began as a one-story gambrel cottage. In 1800, an ell was added for a kitchen, and in 1847, the roof was raised and a second story was added. Next door is the millinery shop of Miss E.F. Hoye, at 238 Main Street.

This seemingly twentieth-century Dutch Colonial, the home of Kenneth and Judith Kolek of 9 Angle Street, was originally the second Slack Tavern (see page 82). The frame of the tavern, built c. 1803, was moved up Cottage Street to Angle Street in 1914 when the extension of School Street from Main Street to Broadway forced its removal. All the dismantled parts were used to rebuild the interior, second floor, attic, and roof. The old bricks were used to veneer the face. The old tavern door has been refitted into the rebuilt house. The Lafayette Room, used to entertain General Lafayette in 1824, is intact today, being incorporated as the front parlor. The much-modified second Slack Tavern is extant today at 9 Angle Street.

John Blake Read (1801-1862) built this Greek Revival-Italianate home in 1842 at 97 Walcott Street, where he lived with his wife, Jane Thacher Ingraham (1809-1903), and his daughter, Mary Drown Read (1829-1858). Mary married Edward LeFavour and had a son, John Edward LeFavour (1858-1911). John and his wife continued to live here until his death. Joseph Ott of the Royal Weaving Company bought the house in 1915 and raised the roof. In the 1930s, Ott's son remodeled again. Today it is the residence of the pastor of the Greek church on the grounds. This is a rare view showing the original design. Note the purple-martin birdhouse on the front lawn.

Jane Thacher (Ingraham) Read enjoys a new gas lamp in her sitting room at 97 Walcott Street in 1901.

This house at 116 Division Street was built by Patrick Dempsey, saloon keeper. This view is from 1913, when the house was owned by the Perry Family, who lived here until 1942. To the left can be seen the home of well-known Pawtucket veterinarian, Dr. Edward Cole. The tower of the old Prospect Street Fire Station can be seen in the distance.

The Varnum T. Barber house, built in 1900-1901 at 9 Beech Street, was constructed for a superintendent at the Slater Cotton Company. It is a two-and-one-half story, Late Victorian dwelling. It has a stepped, cross-gabled roof, castellated corner tower, and an arcaded and battlemented one-story porch on the front side. (Photograph by Bill Gucfa.)

Going home is not always easy! The Blizzard of 1978 stopped traffic for almost a week on Route I-95 North at the Broadway and Cottage Street exits. (*Times* photograph.)

Acknowledgments

Most of the photographs and other illustrations in this book come from the collections of the Spaulding House Research Library and the Pawtucket Public Library. Where no credit line accompanies a picture, it is implied that the source is the Spaulding House Research Library collection. Pictures from the Pawtucket Public Library collection are so designated.

The Times has also generously allowed us to copy and use a number of their archive photographs, and these pictures are credited. *Times* photographers, when known, are acknowledged within the photograph captions.

We are fortunate to have had gifts to our collections from many people. A number of these appear in this book. The following list acknowledges the donors and indicates the pages on which their pictures appear (when two photographs appear on a page, images at the top are designated "T," and those on the bottom are marked "B") We give appreciative thanks to: The Pawtucket Mutual Insurance Company (10T, 10B); Mrs. Frederic R. Morse (Sylvia) (14T, 14B); Elizabeth (Smith) Thresher (18T); Mrs. Earl Dumin (22B); Susan (Leach) Reed (24T); Deborah (Fleming) Charron (24B, 113B); the William K. Toole Company (26T, 26B); Mabel (Tingley) Woolley (27, 39B); Kenneth Roberts (28T, 28B); Leo C. Clark Jr. (29T); Bernard McCaughey Sr. (33T, 33B, 94T); Jannell Truck & Trailer Company (37); Polly (Davis) Stiles (39T, 58T); the New England Tractor Training School (53B); Edwin B. McDermott (58B); Frances L. Smith, historian, Woodlawn Baptist Church (65); Mayor Robert E. Metivier (74/75); Rhode Island Historic Preservation Commission (93B); Virginia (Eddy) Brown (94B, 99T); Catherine (Lovely) Smith (100B); Ruth (Kent) Hatch (102T); Dennis P. McGuire (104); Nino Calabro (106); Pawtucket & Providence Precision Team (109B); Bill Mulholland (114B); Mrs. Chester R. Nichols Jr. (Beryl) (115T); Clare and Brian McKinnon (115B); Jean (Fanion) Kozatek (118T); Preservation Society of Pawtucket (123T); and Susan (LeFavour) Kraus (125T, 125B).

Special thanks for valuable contributions go to Mrs. Agnes Piasecki and John T. Thresher, *Times* librarian.